THE DEVIL'S PLAYGROUND

SABAHUDIN HADZIALIC

Transcendent Zero Press

Houston, TX

Copyright © 2017, Sabahudin Hadzialic

Transcendent Zero Press
www.transcendentzeropress.org

All rights reserved. No part or parts of this book may be reproduced in any format without the expressed written consent of Transcendent Zero Press, or of the author Sabahudin Hadzialic.

ISBN-10:1-946460-91-5
ISBN-13:978-1-946460-91-2

Library of Congress Control Number: 2016933022

Printed in the United States of America

Transcendent Zero Press 16429 El Camino Real Apt. 7 Houston, TX 77062

Cover design by Glynn Monroe Irby
Cover drawing by Dustin Pickering, 2016 (markers and colored pencil)
Majority of the poems were translated by Anya Reich and some of them by Sabahudin Hadzialic

The Devil's Playground

Sabahudin Hadzialic

TABLE OF CONTENTS

TEN YEARS LATER / 7
REALITY FILMED / 8
STRANGE DREAM / 10
…ETERNAL DREAMS / 11
PEN BROTHERS / 12
TO BRANKO MILJKOVIC AND BRANKO COPIC / 13
BRANIMIR STULIC - JOHNNY (the 60's generation) / 14
DEVIL'S PLAYGROUND / 15
ENDLESS LOVE / 16
ANANAS AND BANANA / 17
TO BE MYSELF now and here / 18
FINAL SOLUTION / 19
COPY PASTE / 20
STATES, PARDON ME, CITIES / 21
ANANAS AND BANANA / 22
BLUES FOR MY EX-COUNTRY/HOMELAND / 23
COUNTRY SONG / 24
IF ONLY I WERE YOUNGER / 25
DAYBREAK SOMETIME IN THE FUTURE / 26
AN UNUSUAL POEM / 27
DÉJÀ VU / 28
CONTROL FREAK / 29
CONTRADICTION IN ITSELF / 30
GODS AND SPIRITS / 31
BOSNIA AND HERZEGOVINA / 32
ANNO DOMINI 2009
BOSNIA I HERZEGOVINA / 33
(1990 – 2009)
AN ODD THOUGHT IN GAETA / 34
TO MY CHILDREN / 35
NOISE (from a notebook of a Nutter) / 36
IF YOU EVER GET THE CHANCE…THE TRUTH / 38
BOSNIA (AND HERZEGOVINA) 2030 / 39
BOHEMIAN SOUL / 40
WE DON'T HAVE ANY HOPE HERE / 41
FORMER / 42
HUSH, HUSH…MY DEAR Snow White / 43
DON'T EVEN TRY… / 45
MARGARITAS ANTE PORTAS / 46

LOVELESS / 47
WHO AM I? / 48
A CRY, AGAIN…! / 50
POEM AND WORDS / 51
MUDROST…WISDOM / 52
LOST SOULS / 53
MORNING, METONYMY / 54
FACEBOOK AND THE SEA / 56
THE UNFORGETTABLE LIGHTNESS OF HOPE / 57
NEVER / 58
WHO AM I? / 59
NOT GUILTY! / 60
PERPETUM MOBILE IN THE BALKANS / 61
THE MASTER AND MARGARITA OF 21ST CENTURY / 62
GOOD NIGHT SONG / 63
DAMN BALKANS / 64
THE POET AND FOX / 65
DAMNED DÉJÀ VU (There is no other way out) / 66
MARE NOSTRUM / 67
ONCE UPON TIME / 68
LOVE DREAMS / 69
DESPERATION BREADS LIFE TO THE MOST HONOURABLE DEEDS / 70
AND I AM A PART OF THE JIG-SAW / 71
THE MOTHER OF ALL POEMS / 72
SHE AND…HE / 73
TO HIM, AND US…AS WELL / 74
IT COULD HAVE BEEN BETTER / 75
TRUTH / 76
A NIGHTMARE / 77
INVISIBILITY OF BEING / 78
UNAUTHENTIC POETS / 79
SUBLIME INTERACTION / 80
…IMPRINTS / 81
THE CONSCIOUS, AND OTHERS / 82
TIME TO WONDER / 83
HAPPY DEATH / 84
LIFE / 85
REFLECTION OF POSSIBILITY / 86
THE RIVER OF DREAMS / 87
REPETICIO EST MATER STUDIORUM / 88

FRAGMENTS OF MY MEMORY / 90
VICE VERSA / 91
LIVING IN 'THE DREAMS' STREET / 92
TITO - PARTY, YOUTH - ENGAGEMENT / 93
OAFS GET TO SIT IN THE FRONT ROW / 94
DESTINY OF BOSNIA (as well as HERZEGOVINA) / 95
FRESHNESS / 96
RESURRECTION / 97
PRESENT vs. FUTURE / 98
DREAMT NIGHT / 99
SARAJEVO NOW…AND THEN / 100
VICE VERSA / 101
SPRINT ! / 103
FEET / 104
AWAKENING / 105
NEBULA OF THE SOUL / 106
SHE…THE POEM / 107
AGORA / 108

TEN YEARS LATER

Envy and malice
feed on
my mistakes.
I try to understand
what they are
painlessly looking for
the collectiveness
of my being.
I don't understand
that without pain
there is no life
let alone.....

REALITY FILMED

Dismal image
of my own imprint in time
that's real
inside the vision that- isn't,
is desperately in search for
Her !
...
Queen Elizabeth,
Chatherine, Nikolajevna,
Princess Dianna,
Fatima
Disappear in front of the eyes
of wild hordes.
...
I remain alone
trembling with trepidation
trying to figure out
what is it that they want.
...
Virtual reality of a surreal film-world
is nothing more than
a treacherous impersonation of a real world
that deceives me
a Servile Servant !

..
She's gone !
Will she ever come back ?
The question is swept by the wind.
...

I'll wait for the storm to calm
and try to catch the mistral wind to find a cove,
and search for the place where I met her.
Barefoot and naked.
Back in the day.
On the stage !

STRANGE DREAM

Hands buried in sand
Deep
.....
Blood stained hands.
Both.
...
I try to reach the bottom of the sand pit
digging deep,
feeling pain.
....
Two blue eyes
deep dive
towards you.

Blood shot eyes.
Both.

Carried on the wave of desperate tears,
I try to catch a glimpse of you,
however
you disappeared behind a horizon.
...
Alas !

You drew near, furtively
and embraced
The World !

...ETERNAL DREAMS

I call out her name
at night
while she is asleep.
...

The reflexion of probability
is out of grasp
of my mortal soul
because
Ariadne
spun a yarn
from a molten core.
...
My core!
...
I call out her name
at dawn,
while she is asleep.

She is strong in her
restraint
while she lolls
on the tombstone
in the graveyard
of
my...

...

Destiny.

PEN BROTHERS
(the poem dedicated to Alija Keba and Sabahudin Hadzialic)

The two of us
from the same tribe
from the same seed
the two of us
walk the battlefield
skilfully brandishing
the sword.. of time.

The two of us
from the same kinship
seven high-seas and one ocean
we are the verse keepers
we are the time keepers
and they sing in the name of our freedom.

The two of us
from the same tribe
pen brothers.
Spark created by passion
and times made us
rip the body
from heart to bottom.

Samir Tahirovic, the poet
Donji Vakuf
1st September 2009

TO BRANKO MILJKOVIC AND BRANKO COPIC

Splashed
by its own soul
a man's face
a new face
feebly
puts off
his
deadly fate.

They (he)
doesn't expect
to find peace
it their (his) hopes
and
they (he)
dissolves into void.
Death and Life
are the two sides
of the same coin.
As we understand it...
And what's next?
To be continued
in another life.

BRANIMIR STULIC – JOHNNY (the 60's generation)

Johnny's songs were about the Balkans.
...

True to himself
Johnny tapped into
undreamt dreams.
...
Am I singing.... or am I crying?

I can't figure out
how to run towards the destiny.
Johnny ran away.
Never to return.
...
Or is it just an impression?!

DEVIL'S PLAYGROUND

They understood !

They didn't ask
...
...for anything else
but just a possibility to survive
within the boundaries
of a precious vision.

Vision of world
without hatred and senseless schemes
living in the minds of their neighbours.
...

They understood !

They didn't ask...
...
...for anything else
but just a hope
that a right to live
is a right of every human.

And humanity
remained where it always was.
...
Entrapped within the boundaries
lacking identity.

Today
the life for them is about
survival
and
waiting for the end.
Are they there yet ?

ENDLESS LOVE

In a flash

awareness

brought about enormous pain

when

he realised

that in her

he recognised

reflection

of himself.

ANANAS AND BANANA

Through this poem
I'd like to tell you
that I know
how much I love you.
...
Through this poem
I'd like to tell you
that I want
you to be mine.
...
Through this poem
I'd like to tell you
that I can hold you tight.
...
I'd like...
however I can't deal with it.
How can I have you, love you and hold you
How, when I can't afford
to carry on caring for you.

The other ending with positive thoughts
I like it ..
and I am dealing with it
I can have you, love you and hold you
Because I am strong to carry on and keep up with you.

TO BE MYSELF now and here

Reflection in the mirror
... Runs away from me...

Reflection in the mirror
...Remans within my sight...

I hang on. Here
Dissolved. By hope.

FINAL SOLUTION

How to cut Gordian knot
in B(&H)?
...an educated fellow tosses the question over and over
again...
He repeats the question
time and time again
it doesn't tire him
it spans decades,
even centuries.
Bosnia and Herzegovina
is an answer in itself.
...

The question will die out
when B&H is wiped out.

COPY PASTE

I am not guilty !

I only obeyed my party line !

And

this goes on

and on

for centuries.

STATES, PARDON ME, CITIES

In the little town
across the seven seas
lived a small nation.
This nation could fit into one city.
and nowhere else.
At least that's what little nation's Emperor thought.
Pardon, Duke.
And one day some people left the city.
they were the first to leave.
Followed by the second.
And the third.
Emperor, pardon, Duke
was left alone.
...
The name of the city ?
Look around,
perhaps this is a story
of your.. city.

ANANAS AND BANANA

Through this poem
I'd like to tell you
that I know
how much I love you.
...
Through this poem
I'd like to tell you
that I want
you to be mine.
...
Through this poem
I'd like to tell you
that I can carry you.

...
I'd like all of this
however I can't manage
How can I have you, love you and carry you.
How, when I can't afford
to keep up with keeping you.

BLUES FOR MY EX-COUNTRY/HOMELAND

I had a country.
They took it away.
They did not ask for permission.
The very same people who
now
want to establish
customs zones,
introduce joint parliament sitting
and start to exchange war criminals.
The very same
THEY
who caused the trouble in the first place.
...
I can only say
one word
COUNTRY/HOMELAND
One day you will realise
that
PEOPLE lived there for generations
and not... NO, DON'T SHOOT !!

COUNTRY SONG

Speculation
revives
reminiscence
of the moments of destiny
in my dreams.
I really don't know
why this title ?
When I want
to say something completely opposite
aiming to speak of
unspoken,
unheard of,
and
unthinkable
At least today,
now and here.
Elite culture
is nothing else but
the wish of marginalised people
to establish the rule of impossible
in this corner of the world.
Let them live with it.
Off I go the soul-brothel
I'm off to the pub !

IF ONLY I WERE YOUNGER

I read

Poetry

written by the young poets...

I

don't know

if I should

call it

Regressive or Progressive ?
...

I better shut up

and continue reading

The poetry written by young writers.

BDAYBREAK SOMETIME IN THE FUTURE

It is too hot

to dream

However...

It is to cold

to think

AN UNUSUAL POEM

"I don't know if I can survive
 the night,
 another one in the string
 of my hopes
 because tomorrow is never going to come
 and it is interminably
 delayed
 How?
 Through my disappearance
 from this life,
 without the people.
 Why?
 You ask too much
 and dream too little.
 Of Whom?
 Neither of you or me"
An Ink said to a Pen.

DÉJÀ VU

The balcony was where
it always used to be.
High,
High above me.
There was no light.
Just a flash,
And…

CONTROL FREAK

While
sipping a glass of white
wine
whiteness splashes
...
Sarajevo
engulfed
in a November day.

In what ?
...

In longing
of an accidental sufferer
trying to dash his sadness.

No way.
She doesn't let him.
...
She even controls

his yearning.

CONTRADICTION IN ITSELF

Tenderly

I gaze at her body

and suppress my desire.

What do I desire ?

My own being.

In her.

For me,

and above all

for her.

GODS AND SPIRITS

I don't know
how to survive
my own death !?
She is coming closer
wanting to suck in
21 grams
of my Soul!
...
Did you know
that at the very moment when we die
we are 21 grams lighter ?
21 grams of our Soul!
...
Instantly I feel much better
because
21 grams
remain
as a part of energy field
stronger than death itself.
God ?
Perhaps, if the God exists

BOSNIA AND HERZEGOVINA
ANNO DOMINI 2009

I feel sorry for you

because YOU ARE !

Because of me

who turned into I AM NOT !

Today in the country

that IS and ISN'T.

These are only two words

of hopeless hopes !

Not because of the Country

the Country is no more.

Except the Country's Name

I can't see

Any meaningful meaning.

At least because of you and me

Who ARE and I AM NOT

BOSNIA AND HERZEGOVINA (1990 – 2009)

For years on end
twilight reins
while
night is yet to fall.
I crave night
because
twilight is dying,
slowly.
Night
hasn't fallen yet.
Doesn't know how.

AN ODD THOUGHT IN GAETA

Yet another summer

seeps through my pores
...
The spring departs

as if it never were.

And

I exist

in me

because

of you.

My existence is You.

TO MY CHILDREN

My dear daughter

My dear son

You will touch the horizons of hope

When

The wish turns into a choice...

When

Knowledge overpowers the agony of long search

When

The experience wins a battle over stranded thoughts

When

You realise that my life

Is nothing else

But a bridge built for you to reach your aim.

... Aim ?...

Yes, aim...

Something that only you can make out

and identify with.

To Amer and Sabina

NOISE (form a notebook of a Nutter)

Not in my
Head...
Not in m veins
Where ?
In you !

IF YOU EVER GET A CHANCE....THE TRUTH
(Audiatur et altera pars)

You can't tell the difference

Between

this truth and other truths.
...
It hurts,

They can forgive you anything,

Everything

except success.

BOSNIA (AND HERZEGOVINIA) 2030
(from Tin Soldier digital diary)

They do not lie
There is no one around to lie to !
...
They do not hide
There is no one to hide from !
...
They do not live
There is no one to live for !
...
They are Sodom and Gomorrah of

Our dreams

Our beliefs

Our hopes.

Now !

BOHEMIAN SOUL

My lifeless soul
wanders.
....
If you stumble upon it
stay away.
...

Throw a stone.
Perhaps two.
...

If you miss,
I will never forgive you !

WE DON'T A HAVE ANY HOPE HERE

I don't want
To be enslaved
even to myself.
...
I want
To spend the rest of my life
Wondering
While I'm dying to quench my thirst for hope
If it is possible to have hope
while living in this wasteland...
With no morals, no ethics, no spirit.
The country the size of Lilliput...
... Bosnia(and Herzegovina) ?
I will not search for the answer,
as you, my dear reader, know it already
If only you could understand it...

FORMER

Memory
fades
while verbs in its present continuous form
swell in my head.
Her ghost
lingers on the shores of Geneva Lake
thousands light years...ago.
She escaped
the bloody dawns
of ethos.
But I escaped from her.
Although I did not want to.
Again !

HUSH, HUSH .. MY DEAR Snow White

In my scattered dreams
I remember
the fire in her eyes.
...
I did not question
this fairytale character
crafted – by me.
...

The one thing that hurt me
was her image
displayed all over.
...

In the underground stations
and
 drawn on cable-cars.
...

I walked up to
my own shadow
and said:
"I will erase you
 as if you never existed ?!"
She smiled and walked away,
towards the nearest billboard, and said:
'You forget, maestro,
that in the moment of my creation
all your intentions died.
The beauty is in the eye of the beholder.
in this case – the spectator!"

I took the brush
and stabbed the hand that created her.

There you are !

DON'T EVEN TRY...

My poem
is nothing else
but
demented illusion
of this
character
Me
to cast Picasso into Moliere,
...
Pity on him,
Alas !
He doesn't know
that Guernica is the one and only.

We are them,
we are they
...

They
who keep repeating themselves !

MARGARITAS ANTE PORTAS

I am
the reconciliation
of her dreams

...
But her soul
craves peace.

...

The place you are yet to reach,
is the place where your hopes stretch.

...
Hope is the last to die
....

With a bit of luck !

LOVELESS

Her hands

were hanging

somewhere

up in the air

while she was trying

to touch love.
...
Love

reached

her.
...
Love

Touched

her.

WHO AM I ?

Lyrics is dying.

Here.

I don't want to call it any other name

just here.

Because....

Today, anno domini 6 July 2009

the devil knocked on my door

and said

that he was the exclusive owner

of my soul.

I did not protest

I did not run away

I did not drive him away

because

The devil

Was

The reflection of

Myself...
...

Once upon the time

A CRY, AGAIN...!

A sharp December day
cuts through the warmth
of fallen thoughts...
Hers...
and mine...
...
I think that
she forgave me
for
hopeless, distressed
roaming
through the wilderness of her own being.
...
The very next moment
I am thrown
on the used-dreams pile.
...
I wake up
and beg for forgiveness.
...
She turned.
She said:
'Maybe, maybe..."

POEM AND WORDS

Words do not make a verse
 But
A word has the power of a verse

...WISDOM

I am running towards
The Exit
of my narcissist self.

Almost ailing.

I am running towards
The Entrance
of my own death.

and...
I
remain silent all the way through !

...

LOST SOULS

They stand
stuck between
my mind
and...
your mind.

They are
the soldiers-keepers of
my destiny
and
your fortune.

They are
a miserable memory of
of their own manifestation...

mine
and
yours.

Who are they ?!
They are
You and Me.

MORNING, METONYMY

This morning
wherever I looked
there were snails everywhere.

The meandering rivers
like a giant anaconda
flew
freely
while the blue clad uniformed officer
asked for signature
... once upon the time.

Poetry
confined in envelope
splashed me.

The Admiral said
that it is our training voyage
and that this is my town
my constellation
the shadow is the real one
and there is grace
we should trust
this morning
as we trust grace.

I recommend
Sabahudin, the poet from Bugojno
alongside Lorca, pipe and Brecht.

He is the shadow
of a sleepy Whisper in the Dark
enshrined in plural.
He is an underground stream.
He stands

He evolves
He disappears.

Oh, my friends
if I don't believe you
what then, what ?

Will Posiedon, the Earth Shaker
turn out today ?

Amir Brka, the poet
Tesanj, 8th August 2000

FACEBOOK AND THE SEA

Thirty five degrees centigrade
and my soul is still frozen.
...
The sea and the sun
are just another two excuses
to escape reality.
...
When I can't
log into my Facebook...
...

THE UNFORGETTABLE LIGHTNESS OF HOPE

Can't they realise
that arousing is under way ?

They don't' understand that reality is harsh.

Can't they realise
that
they will ultimately perish.
...
Unless
we continue to stuff up
again and again.

We have been trying since 1990
and failed.

We muddled up
time and time again.

NEVER

The music of my youth
slowly
trickles down the cracks
of bizarre illusions.
Is this
the destiny
or just a flutter
of bogus hopes ?
...
Nevertheless
I assume
that I may become an artist
only if I am human.

....

Not just any artist
but human
form another universe !

WHO AM I ?

In this part of the world

poetry is dying.
I don't want to say 'in this country'.

Today, anno domini 6th July 2009
The devil came through the door
and just said
that my soul belongs to him
and no one else.

I didn't think twice
I didn't run away
I didn't resist
The devil – it was me…
…
Long time ago.

NOT GUILTY

It was nice
to think
and finally learn
that he was not guilty !
...

And he wasn't.

What is guilt after all
but interposed image
of distorted thought
that he was guilty.
And perhaps he
wasn't guilty at all.

The accusers
are guilty folks.

Guilt breeds guilt.
His
Theirs, as well.

PERPETUM MOBILE IN THE BALKANS

I stepped/entered
into backyard/patio
and
had coffee/Turkish coffee/espresso
with my neighbour/fellow citizen.

Then/after
I took a pistol/revolver
and
shot myself/put a bullet
through my head !?

Language does not fire bullets
however the words you use can end your life.

THE MASTER AND MARGARITA OF 21st CENTURY

Heat
of my own vanity
sneaks into
entangled pores
of my degeneration.
....
All aboard !
Shouts
the black cat
while the streetcar named desire
cuts off
the imbecile's head.

My life
is too short
to grasp
that I have not lived at all !

GOOD NIGHT SONG

I never dreamt
that I would have a break down.
...
Until the night
when I saw her
singing
all alone
pale
and
pretty.
The good night song.
While she was looking
through
the photo album from our wedding.
I joined her singing.
Without uttering a sound.
Two meters under
ground.

DAMN BALKANS

I stepped on
my left foot
this morning !
You wonder how I know ?
I lost my right foot
to the land mine
laid during the war.
Phew !

THE POET AND FOX

What is poetry,
My dear Ujevic?
... asked one fox
in the city of Mostar,
while the fox slowly
poured plum brandy
home made
from the bottle
into quite small
brandy glass...
and half filled it.
....
Tin looked at the fox
and through smile
said:
...it is fuller,
than this glass,
but oh my Lord,
it is peculiar,
my dear Omer...!."

DAMNED DÉJÀ VU (There is no other way out)

Warmth
day by day
embraces
my soul.

The year
is
2060.
and
I
am not
there
because
I
became
happy
only
when
my
body
rested.

MARE NOSTRUM

Her love

stayed at the back of my mind

like an imprint

of bare feet

in the sand.

Swept by the sea.

Swept by the time.

The waves of time

swept the shores interminably

while I walked along,

and

The words stuck.

Because of love.

Her love.

... Nevertheless

ONCE UPON TIME

Obeying
I don't want to be
without chance
to pass the rite of
becoming a human
through grief.

Angry
I don't want to be
without chance
to fence the dreams without me
through a mistake.

Submissive
I don't want to be
without chance
to hurt the love I think it is...
...
But, I do all of that.
No regrets.
I am human.
Hurt.
Because of you.

LOVE DREAMS

Once upon a time

I dreamt of love.

I awoke into nothingness.

In love.

DESPERATION BREADS LIFE TO THE MOST HONOURABLE DEEDS

A friend of mine
Confided in me today
That desperation
breads my inspiration.

I just said
That was nicely put
if it were not for him
I wouldn't have recalled at all
the bitter sting
(of desperation)

AND I AM A PART OF THE JIG-SAW

It feels so good

to watch your own reflection

mirrored in destiny.

While it disappears

under a surge

of odd

barbarians.

They looked just fine

when taken on the face value.

And the story goes on

until they splashed their cards on the table.

Mimicking yet again

not only myths

but written legends.

THE MOTHER OF ALL POEMS

Thirty years ago

I wrote my first poem.

At least I thought

that it was a poem...

I still write

poems...
...
And I still think

that

I am writing
...
poems !

SHE AND... HE

Happy chap
spearheads towards destiny
while in the land of hectic hopes.
He doesn't turn back...
...He doesn't pay attention
to the thump of troublesome waves
made by
inhumane chaps
who silently
try to
turn
their malicious,
double-faced,
envious,
hateful,
standards
into his reality.
...
He does not want
at all
to wake up
through self reflection.
...
He.
...
She is there.
She is his mate.
The one and only.

And she walks away
with him.
No turning back.

TO HIM, AND US.... AS WELL

The years
behind me
make me strong
despite of
my inner weakness.
...
His reflection
shines
entwined between the thoughts
of focused hopes
because
what is life
but just a strange thought
within His desire
to rebuild himself
...
In us
he can
find
...

IT COULD HAVE BEEN BETTER

My dreams
are still hanging
at the tip of the dagger
of my dreams.
Sobbing, grief-stricken
wanting to
turn into Reality.
No,
that is not to happen.
The culprit is no one
but me.
Why ?
The answer, my friend,
was swept away
by the river of Wisdom.
Not mine, the least.....

TRUTH

Through a pale image
I couldn't discern
 wrath
 worthy of strange astonishment.
...
Wrath ?
...
Yes, because humanity
Only craves
Lust
For something madden
For something untouched
For something undreamt of...
...
What ?

The life itself.

A NIGHTMARE

Rage
soars
carried on the waves of destiny.
...
I do not believe
what I see.
...
I look away
while
she is finding comfort
in ruffling through my hair.
....

I've woken up
It is bloody hot
in Bahamas.
Unlike Sarajevo.

INVISIBILITY OF BEING

She did not give a damn
For staying with me.

?
The ashes

UNAUTHENTIC POETS

Once upon the time
I searched for myself
in you.

I was yet to realise
that unauthentic poets
hang around waiting
for the seagull to perish.
...

I can't let them triumph.
...

And not because of me.

...

Because of you.

I am neither
the important one
Nor...
the ideal one.

They are
the illusion
of their own intention.

And me?

I am the reality

of your core.

SUBLIME INTERACTION

She survived
amongst endless whispers
although
She was vocal.

...

She became quiet
although
She was wide awake.

...

She bared her soul in a fit of rage
although
She is hope.

....

She survived the sun blaze
although
I left her to burn.

...

She did not hold it against me
although
She just smiled and left.
Without me.

... IMPRINTS

Troubled by
the reality of today
I retreat in the past
Wasn't the life better then ?
...In the memory of the past...
The clouds disperse
under the rays of hope.
Under our skies
the awakening
is always stained with blood.

THE CONSCIOUS, AND OTHERS

Cynicism
lures in their veins.
...
Hypocrisy
is their Anthem
while
misery of others
is their intertwined desire.
...

I plead with you
Do not wipe out Consciousness
You, the Others !

TIME TO WONDER

Crimson leaves
October leaves
Traceless leaves
dancing
basking in the rays of hope…
Autumn
now knocking at the door
will not leave a trace in your eyes.
…

Trace worth of a wonder.
….
Trace that I need so badly.
…
No !

The time
stopped
so
that
it
could
start
trickling
again…

HAPPY DEATH

I left her
on the side-line of my memories,
just a girly face
is what I remember.
She left
with a big smile
when the sensual joy
illuminated my face.
Typical ending, isn't it ?
It's the way of life.

LIFE

There are times

when I don't feel like breathing.

She takes in breath

for me.

REFLECTION OF POSSIBILITY

Never run away from me...

Being resolute as I am
I may not forgive you.
...
 I can't endure the strain,
...
Ariadne's thread

THE RIVER OF DREAMS

Her words
are submersed
in the river of my dreams...

It is neither the Nile,
nor the Mississippi,
not even the Danube
and let alone the Volga...

Her words
are twirl
of unfulfilled hopes...

Mine...
and
hers...

REPETICIO EST MATER SUTDIORUM

Warmth
of time and space
is nothing else
but unforgettable lightness
of bizarre rhymes
that reverberate
among twisted corridors of my soul.

...

Chilliness of déjà vu
and space
is nothing else
but
bizarre form
of odd expectations
that sway embarrassingly
to the rhythm of her tambourine.
...

They dance.
Without us.

...

Long time ago
the two of us
got lost in insanity.
My insanity.
Hoping that
she will say NO to this madness.

....

That was it.

...

Encircled by a wall, in hope

FRAGMENTS OF MY MEMORY

The temperature
is rising
in the heart of
lost hopes.

The temperature
is falling
in the heart of
frenzied expectations
and future impressions.

It all disappeared
with a bang.

It was created
with a bang.
...
In a bang
of hazy destiny.

VICE VERSA

Tender darkness
reverberates disdainfully.

Crisp light
gravitates tenderly.

Everything will be just fine
...
like wilt buds of faith
....
If I only knew

that through words

I can express truth

and not lie

to myself.

And you !

LIVING IN 'THE DREAMS' STREET

Don't turn into
a shadowy street.

You can easily get lost.

There are
one way and two way
streets
Like people
sometimes spotless
sometimes grubby
and
sometimes just a dead end.

TITO – PARTY, YOUTH – ENGAGEMENT

Once upon the time there was One and Only.
HE.
Today there are Many.
THEM.
Tomorrow there will be No One.
US.

OAFS GET TO SIT IN THE FRONT ROW

My destiny lined
by sunset.

My idea escapes
forever.

I'm not guilty.

I didn't ask for pardon.

I'm not guilty.

Can I really change ?

Please them.

No, I don't want to run away...
... I want to dream...

DESTINY OF BOSNIA
(as well as HERZEGOVNA)

I woke up in the arms of a nightmare.
I dreamt of innocence and future.

I walked, shrouded in astonishment.

Stuck in the mud, shattered to core.
Drowned in mediocrity.

I took off, shrouded in astonishment.

I believed that I am – now and here.
I was – then and there.

I lied, shrouded in astonishment.

Motivated by strength and · survived
Became human – submissive and merciful.

I dashed away, shrouded in astonishment.

Why, what's the purpose ?

I keep wondering.

Still.

FRESHNESS

I gazed at
decaying skeleton.

There were no stars.

And I...?
I was breathing my last breath.
But I didn't know how to die.

RESURRECTION

Fully awake

raw reality

is an obstacle

to my coming.
...
It was easier

before 2000.

There were

the Believers.

PRESENT VS. FUTURE

It's cold....

It's frosty...

It's hot...

It's hope...

DREAMT NIGHT

Yesterday I dreamt about night.
Appreciation of night.
And dreams.

SARAJEVO NOW ....AND THEN

Morning

in Sarajevo

was murky

this year as the year before.

Like my soul

on this

drizzly and dim

evening

hanging around.

Cold, June evening.

Morning.

Tomorrow, as well.

VICE VERSA

Cosy darkness

Resonates chilly.

Chilliness

light

gravitate towards

warmth.

And everything

Would be just fine
...
Like withered flowers of faith
....
If only

I knew

that

I am able to express the truth.

And not lie

To me

and You !

SPRINT !

I was running towards you
I did it for me
...

You were running towards me
You did it for you

...
I can't get
Why we were running away from each other
And did it for us.

Remark: All of those poems of Sabahudin Hadzialic above were translated by <u>Anya Reich</u>

The next were translated only by Sabahudin Hadzialic:

FEET

Within the twilight of my memories
footprint of hers resurrections

I am struggling on the run
not getting

The pain is immeasurable
My fault

infatuated

I continue to pray

and love

because she is always here

remains

resuscitate.

AWAKENING

Reflection
of my own madness
is shining
within the night of my restlessness.
Treating the cries
of human dreams
I cannot do alone.
With whom I will?
And when?

NEBULA OF THE SOUL

I am enlightening the hell of daffodils
while disappearing in loss
of the sense...
me.

Fighting for the incarnation
of the soul is
wooing with the nebula

Whether will survive...the soul?

Or disappear among rocks,
cliffs,
of searching.

Aspiring towards the fall.

SHE...THE POEM

The poem about her
decanted with my tears
through decades
arises

And, within the time of blenching
light flashes
through the distance and intention...

The poem disappeared
with return of her.

Am I wrong,
Or she is my
...poem?

AGORA[1]

The place
of personalization of the direct
democracy
and the starting end
of civilization.
Wondering value of try
within the announcement
of disappearance of the species.
Two thousand years
Later.
Today.
Us.

---

[1] *The **agora** (Ancient Greek: Ἀγορά, Agorá) was a central spot in ancient Greek city-states. The literal meaning of the word is "gathering place" or "assembly". The agora was the center of athletic, artistic, spiritual and political life of the city*

ABOUT THE AUTHOR

Sabahudin Hadžialić was born in Mostar, Bosnia and Herzegovina, Europe. He is a member of the Bosnia and Herzegovina Association of Writers (Sarajevo, BiH), Croatian Writers Association Herzeg Bosnia (Mostar, BiH), Association of Writers Serbia (Belgrad, Serbia), Association of Writers of Montenegro (Podgorica, Montenegro) and Journalists Association of Bosnia and Herzegovina, Association of Independent Intellectuals "Circle 99", Sarajevo and Ambassador of POETAS del MUNDO in Bosnia and Herzegovina. He is Freelance Editor in Chief of the electronic and print magazine DIOGEN pro culture and Editor in Chief of E–magazine MaxMinus from Sarajevo, Bosnia and Herzegovina. He has the status of the self-sustained artist in the Canton of Sarajevo since Jan. 1, 2009. As of Jan. 1, 2013 he has a status of distinguish self-sustained artist in Canton of Sarajevo by the Decision of the Minister of Culture and Sport of the Canton. He writes poetry and prose with the editing and reviewing books of other authors. He has published 16 books of poetry and prose (stories, aphorisms, stage plays, novels) and essays in Bosnia and Herzegovina, Serbia, France, Italy and Switzerland. Since school year 2011/2012 he works as part-time teacher (Assoc. Prof.) on IUT - International University Travnik (BiH), Faculty of Media and Communications. He has a Master's of Science (MSc.) in Media and Communications and he is a doctor of IUT. He is International Relations Coordinator as well as Coordinator of IUT Institutes. He is the member of International boards of several scientific and cultural magazines in BiH and internationally. So far he published several scientific papers in national and international scientific journals. He is author of scientific papers, articles, and bibliography and reviews articles published in domestic and foreign magazines. He has participated in numerous international and national scientific conferences. His poems, short stories, stage plays, novel and aphorisms have been published in both national and international journals. His poetry and prose were translated into numerous languages. He was the co-owner of the first private newspaper in Socialist Republic of Bosnia and Herzegovina (as part of former Yugoslavia) titled "POTEZ", Bugojno, Bosnia and Herzegovina back in 1990.

This biography was taken and revised by
www.eurasiareview.com/author/sabahudin-hadzialic/

www.ingramcontent.com/pod-product-compliance
Lightning Source LLC
Chambersburg PA
CBHW071233090426
42736CB00014B/3064